Ogden, Utah:
Greatest Place on Earth?

Unveiling the Irresistible Allure of America's Best-Kept Secret

By Micah Wells

"In every walk with nature, one receives far more than he seeks."
— *John Muir*

Copyright © 2023

Table of Contents

Dedication

This book is lovingly dedicated to the vibrant community and enduring spirit of Ogden, Utah. To the locals who have welcomed me with open arms, the friends I've made along the way, and the untold stories waiting to be discovered—thank you for making Ogden the greatest place on Earth.

To my family, for always being my own personal 'greatest place,' no matter where we are in the world. Your support and love have been the backbone of this journey.

And finally, to you, the reader, for embarking on this adventure through Ogden with me. May you find your own reasons to call this city great, and may your life be enriched by its countless charms.

See you on the trails, in the cafes, or under the starry Ogden sky.

Micah Wells

Introduction: "Why Ogden? Why Not!"

Hello, you curious wanderer, intrepid adventurer, or perhaps, the uninitiated skeptic who picked up this book with the weighty question: Is Ogden, Utah really the greatest place on Earth? Well, fasten your seatbelt because you're about to embark on a joyride through a place that's as unique as its name.

First of all, let me extend a warm, hearty welcome to all of you who are about to discover the myriad wonders of Ogden. For those who are already "in the know," you might find yourselves nodding along, saying, "Yep, that's my Ogden!"

So, what's the deal with this city tucked away in the Wasatch Range? Is it the jaw-dropping natural beauty? The exquisite food scene? The eclectic mix of history and hip? The answer, my friends, is a resounding YES to all of the above, and so much more!

If you're one of those people who like your travel destinations to be Instagram-worthy, then Ogden is your place. Picture-perfect landscapes? Check! Quaint, cobblestone streets bursting with character? Double-check! A burgeoning art scene that would make any Brooklynite go "Woah!"? Triple check!

But hang on! Ogden isn't just a feast for your eyes and taste buds; it's a veritable smorgasbord of experiences that touch the soul and invigorate the mind. Imagine a place where you can hit the slopes in the morning, enjoy an artisan coffee in the afternoon, and attend a film festival by evening. Sounds too good to be true? That's Ogden for you!

Consider this book your all-access pass, your VIP ticket, your backstage pass to everything that makes Ogden a hidden gem just begging to be discovered. We'll explore Ogden's lush landscapes, delve into its rich history, shimmy through its nightlife, and perhaps, even whisper some of its best-kept secrets.

Is Ogden the greatest place on Earth? Well, I won't spill the beans just yet, but let's just say, by the end of this journey, you might find yourself browsing through real estate listings and planning your move. And if you're already here, well, aren't you the lucky one?

So put on your adventure cap, grab a snack (you'll need the energy for all the excitement), and let's plunge into the irresistible allure of Ogden, Utah.

Chapter 1: "A Mountain for Every Mood"

Welcome back, adventurers! If you made it past the introduction without packing your bags for Ogden, let me tempt you a bit more with the sort of stuff that even fairytales would envy. That's right, we're talking about mountains. But not just any mountains—Ogden's mountains are the crème de la crème, the cherry on top, the sprinkle of magic dust on your ordinary day.

The Beauty and Diversity of Surrounding Landscapes

The Wasatch Range is like the protective big brother of Ogden, standing tall and majestic, keeping an eye out for its vibrant sibling. But these mountains are more than just pretty faces. They're like a moody artist that shows different colors and temperaments depending on the day, the season, or even the hour! Sunrise hikes? Imagine a sky bursting with shades of orange, pink, and purple as if someone tipped over a giant paint bucket on the horizon. Or how about a winter wonderland where the peaks don a cloak of pristine white snow? Absolutely breathtaking!

And let's not forget the valleys, the forests, the lakes! Picture yourself hiking through a densely wooded trail, the leaves forming a natural canopy overhead, the ground beneath your feet springy with rich, earthy soil. Then you emerge from the trees to find a serene mountain lake, its surface so mirror-like you could almost see your future in it. Spoiler alert: Your future says, "Move to Ogden!"

Hiking, Skiing, and Mountain Biking Galore

"Okay, okay," you say. "The mountains are drop-dead gorgeous. But what can I do there?"

Ah, my friend, this is where Ogden shows off its 'fun-for-all-seasons' badge. Are you a fan of hiking? Ogden's got trails that range from 'a leisurely walk in the park' to 'OMG, is this the stairway to heaven?'—there's a route for everyone. Names like Waterfall Canyon, Indian Trail, and Skyline Trail might not mean much to you now, but they'll become your new weekend vocabulary. You'll be the person dropping casual comments like, "Oh, you've never done the Malan's Peak? You absolutely must!"

And skiers, you're in for a treat. Snowbasin and Powder Mountain are the stuff of legends. Picture powdery slopes so inviting that you'd swear they're whispering your name as you ski down in euphoric delight.

"But I'm more of a mountain biker," you say? Well, hang onto your helmets! Ogden's biking trails will make you feel like you're riding a roller coaster built by Mother Nature herself. From beginner-friendly loops to adrenaline-pumping downhill courses, Ogden's got you covered. And the best part? The mountain vistas act as a naturally rejuvenating backdrop, so you'll never feel too tired to go just one more round.

So, there you have it, folks! Whether you're the contemplative hiker, the daredevil skier, or the thrill-seeking biker, Ogden has a mountain that matches your mood, and activities that make your heart sing. A Mountain for Every Mood? More like a lifetime of moods catered for every mountain!

Next up, we'll venture down from the mountains and into the heart of the city, where your taste buds are in for a roller coaster of their own. Ready for the ride to continue? Of course, you are!

Onward, to deliciousness and beyond!

Chapter 2: "Heavenly Aromas & Tantalizing Tastes"

Hey, you foodies out there! Put down your organic, gluten-free, keto-friendly snacks for a moment. We're about to talk about the REAL food, the kind that makes your taste buds dance like they're at a rave and your stomach say, "Thank you, I love you, and can we move to Ogden now?"

You thought Ogden was just mountains and trails? Oh, you're so cute. Let me introduce you to the culinary wonderland that is Ogden, Utah.

A Culinary Journey Through Ogden

Picture this: You wake up to the aroma of freshly brewed coffee wafting from the hipster café down the street. You know, the one with the mustached barista who knows exactly how to make your coffee so that it tastes like liquid happiness. But wait, coffee's just the beginning. We're about to go around the world, all while staying within the cozy bounds of Ogden. Buckle up!

Ever had a sushi burrito? Well, you can in Ogden! How about genuine Mexican food that makes you want to salsa dance with joy? Yep, we've got that too. Authentic Italian, mouth-watering Thai, sumptuous Greek—Ogden is a United Nations of Flavors, all getting along harmoniously on your plate.

But let's not overlook the classic American fare. Burgers that are more stacked than a Jenga tower, BBQ so smoky and tender it could bring a tear to your eye, and farm-to-table offerings that make you feel like the farmer personally delivered it to your plate.

From Food Trucks to Fine Dining

"Whoa, slow down," you might say. "What if I want something quick and easy?" Have no fear, food trucks are here! Parked strategically in spots where you're most likely to get a craving (those sneaky geniuses), Ogden's food trucks serve everything from hand-crafted tacos to gourmet cupcakes. Imagine biting into a steaming bao bun while sitting on a park bench, the mountain peaks saluting you in the distance. Yep, that's an everyday kind of joy in Ogden.

But let's say you're in the mood for something a bit more, ahem, refined. Picture yourself in an elegant dining room, crystal chandeliers above, a panoramic mountain view beyond the window, and a menu that makes you feel like royalty. Whether it's a steak cooked to perfection, a vegan dish that defies all your past assumptions about vegan food, or a seafood entrée that takes you on a trip to coastal heaven, Ogden's got it all. And the best part? You don't need to be a millionaire to dine like one here.

So there you have it—Ogden isn't just a feast for your eyes and soul; it's a literal feast. A place where culinary dreams come true, where every bite tells a story, and where you'll start planning your next meal before you've even finished your first.

Hungry for more? Stay tuned, because our next stop is Ogden's electrifying downtown. The mountains gave you an adrenaline rush, the food fueled your body, and now it's time to nourish your cultural soul.

Grab a napkin, wipe that drool, and let's keep the adventure rolling!

Chapter 3: "Downtown Vibes: Where Hip Meets History"

Alright, cool cats and groovy kittens, it's time to slip into those walking shoes because we're heading downtown! If you thought the mountains were Ogden's showstopper, wait until you experience 25th Street and the bustling hubs that make up this city's beating heart.

25th Street and Beyond

Let's start with 25th Street, shall we? Picture a street that's straight out of a movie set. We're talking vintage marquees, cobblestone pathways, and buildings with that rustic brick charm. You'll find boutiques that feel like treasure troves, filled with artisanal trinkets, handmade crafts, and rare books that smell like history.

Now add some colorful street murals, string lights crisscrossing overhead, and the soft sounds of live music floating through the air. Coffee shops, craft breweries, art galleries—it's like someone took Brooklyn, San Francisco, and New Orleans and mashed them into one irresistible strip of pure, concentrated fun.

Hungry again? (It's okay, we're not judging.) The eateries on 25th Street range from charming cafes that serve up poetic lattes, to gastropubs where you can pair your handcrafted beer with spicy Buffalo cauliflower bites. So much yum in one place—it's unfair to every other street, really.

Merging of History and Modern Culture in Architecture and People

But let's get a bit serious. One of the most captivating things about Ogden's downtown is how it masterfully melds history with hipness. These streets have stories to tell, my friends. Once upon a time, Ogden was a bustling railroad town, a confluence of cultures, ideas, and of course, goods. The Union Station standing grandly at one end of 25th Street is a testament to that era, now transformed into museums and galleries.

Modern buildings and historical structures stand side by side, like old friends having a good chat. And it's not just the architecture—Ogden's people are a vibrant blend of young and old, traditional and avant-garde, laid-back and high-energy.

You'll meet artists passionately doodling on their sketchpads, musicians strumming their guitars in open-air venues, and history buffs who can tell you tales that turn Ogden into a living, breathing storybook.

What's more, events like the Ogden Arts Festival, Farmers Market, and the Twilight Concert Series bring people from all walks of life together. It's a place where you'll strike up conversations with strangers that feel like catching up with old friends.

So, are you feeling the downtown vibes yet? Ogden's 25th Street and its surrounding areas are not just postcard-perfect; they are an experience, a mood, a vibe that you won't find anywhere else.

Chapter 4: "Ogden's Hidden Gems: Unexplored Treasures Await!"

Hey there, explorers! So, you've seen the peaks, savored the eats, and vibed with the streets. You're probably thinking, "I've seen all of Ogden's glory." Oh, you sweet summer child. Just when you think you've got Ogden all figured out, it winks at you and reveals yet another layer. So, put on your metaphorical pirate hats, because we're going on a treasure hunt!

Lesser-Known Places That Only Locals Know

You know how every place has its little secrets, whispered from one local to another like a sacred mantra? Ogden's got those in spades. Let's talk about Mystery Soda Machine, shall we? Situated in an unexpected spot, this soda machine is anything but ordinary. You insert your coin, and voila! A mystery can pops out. Maybe it's your favorite, maybe it's something you've never tried before. The only guarantee is a delightful surprise!

Next, let's head to the hidden alleys of downtown Ogden. Far from dingy or sketchy, these are artistic havens adorned with murals so intricate and vivid, you'll wonder if the walls are about to come alive. Rarely featured on Instagram feeds, this is the real Ogden—the unfiltered, unrehearsed version that you'll fall in love with, over and over again.

Hidden Parks, Obscure Cafes, Tucked-Away Art

If you're in the mood for some alone time, the hidden parks in Ogden offer the serenity of a mountain retreat minus the hike. Take Waterfall Park—a mini-oasis that provides a peaceful backdrop for reading, meditating, or simply catching your breath. It's so tucked away that even Google Maps might give you a wink and say, "Good luck!"

Craving a quiet cup of coffee? Skip the popular spots and visit one of the cozy, obscure cafes where the owner remembers not just your name but also how you like your latte. These places aren't just cafes; they're like your living room, but with better coffee and a dash of Ogden magic.

And let's not forget the art scene. Beyond the galleries and museums lie grassroots art studios, tucked away in corners you'd never expect. From handcrafted jewelry to sculptures made from recycled materials, these artisans are Ogden's unsung heroes, infusing the city with creativity one masterpiece at a time.

So, my adventurous friends, Ogden's allure lies not just in its grand attractions but also in its hidden nooks and crannies. This chapter was like a treasure map, giving you a sneak peek into Ogden's lesser-known wonders. But the real joy lies in discovering them yourself, in turning the corners and stumbling upon unexpected magic.

As for what's next—oh, you won't believe it! We're diving into the community spirit of Ogden. Trust me, you'll want to become a local after this.

Ready for another dose of Ogden awesomeness? Onwards and upwards!

Chapter 5: "Lights, Camera, Ogden! Hollywood's Secret Crush"

Roll out the red carpet, folks, because it turns out our charming Ogden is a bona fide movie star! That's right, Hollywood's been sneaking into our backyard for years, capturing the city's raw beauty, rustic charm, and ever-present aura of "coolness" on the silver screen. We've been in more scenes than a background actor at a soap opera—only Ogden isn't acting. Nope, this city is just naturally fabulous.

Movies and TV Shows Filmed in Ogden

So, where might you have caught a glimpse of Ogden's Hollywood debut? How about the classic film "Con Air," where our unique landscape made an impressive stand-in for an arid desert? Or what about the iconic train scenes in "The Sandlot"? Yep, Ogden was the real MVP there.

TV shows? You betcha! From crime dramas to documentaries, filmmakers just can't seem to stay away from Ogden's picturesque mountains, historic architecture, and magnetic downtown.

In fact, if Ogden were a person, it would have its own star on the Hollywood Walk of Fame by now. It's like the city has its own agent who's really good at negotiating contracts. "You want a dramatic backdrop for your period piece? How about a sunset over our gorgeous Wasatch Range?"

How Ogden Has Always Been a Star, You Just Didn't Know It

But let's not forget the homegrown talent, because Ogden doesn't just look good on camera—it's bursting with stories and characters that could fuel seasons of compelling television. From the storied history of the railroad boom to the modern-day adventurers who scale cliffs and barrel down bike trails, Ogden's inhabitants are as captivating as any A-list celeb.

And don't you think it's oddly fitting? A city this charismatic, with its eye-popping landscapes, mouth-watering eats, and feet-tapping beats, deserves a bit of spotlight. Ogden has always been a star; the world is just starting to catch up.

So, next time you're wandering down 25th Street or exploring a hidden trail, imagine a film crew capturing your every move. In Ogden, you're not just living life; you're starring in a blockbuster hit where the city steals every scene.

Are you starstruck yet? Don't ask for Ogden's autograph; instead, become a part of its unfolding epic saga. And speaking of epic, brace yourselves. The next chapter is all about the legends, myths, and folklore that make Ogden not just a city, but a legend in its own right.

Chapter 6: "When the Sun Goes Down: Nightlife & Entertainment"

Okay, party animals and night owls, this one's for you! We've hiked the mountains, we've brunched like champions, and we've traipsed through cinematic settings. But when the sun dips behind the Wasatch Range, painting the sky with hues of orange and purple, Ogden takes a deep breath, flips its hair, and says, "Alright, let's turn it up a notch!"

Bars, Music, and Nightclubs

First stop—let's talk libations. From craft breweries with flights of beer that feel like a hoppy journey around the world, to speakeasy-style bars where the bartenders muddle, shake, and stir your cocktail to perfection—Ogden's got your thirst covered.

And we haven't even touched on the live music yet. On any given night, you could be tapping your feet to a local jazz band, head-banging to a rock group, or dancing to a DJ spinning records like there's no tomorrow. Places like The Lighthouse Lounge and Funk 'n Dive Bar are not just establishments; they're institutions that define Ogden's soulful, eclectic audio landscape.

But what if you're not in the mood for a bar or a club? How about a rooftop cinema with a view of the twinkling cityscape? Yep, we got that too! And don't get me started on the comedy clubs where you can laugh till your cheeks hurt. Ah, choices, choices!

A Guide to Painting the Town Red, Ogden Style!

So how do you make the most of Ogden's night scene? First, forget the high heels and the neckties. In Ogden, casual is the new black. Wear something you can move in because trust me, you'll want to dance, whether it's on a dance floor or perhaps, spontaneously, on a table.

Next, go with the flow. Ogden's nightlife doesn't come with a strict itinerary; it comes with serendipity. Maybe you'll discover a new band that's playing their first gig, or maybe you'll end up at a bonfire party by the river.

Lastly, and this is important—take a moment to step outside, look up, and breathe. Because in Ogden, the stars seem to shine a little brighter, just like the city itself.

Well, there you have it—a whistle-stop tour of Ogden after dark, a time when the city shakes off its daytime composure and lets its hair down. You've seen Ogden's natural beauty, culinary finesse, historic elegance, cinematic allure, and now, its nocturnal zest. Could this city BE any more perfect? Spoiler: Yes, it can. And we're about to reveal how!

Chapter 7: "Artistic Souls: Galleries, Murals, & Music"

Hey there, lovers of all things beautiful! Ready to unleash your inner artist? Because Ogden is practically a sprawling, open-air gallery where art doesn't just hang on walls—it surrounds you. From murals that redefine street art to galleries that rival big-city exhibits, Ogden's got an artsy vibe that's as palpable as the mountain air.

Ogden's Artsy Side

Let's kick off with Ogden's galleries—curated spaces where local artists display everything from avant-garde sculptures to breathtaking landscapes. Places like The Eccles Art Center aren't just buildings; they're cultural landmarks where you can find pieces that range from abstract to zany.

And if you think you need to be an art connoisseur to appreciate it all, think again! Ogden's art scene is the opposite of snobby; it's inviting and interactive. How else would you explain art walks where galleries throw open their doors for everyone to hop in and out, munching on appetizers while pondering the finer points of brush strokes?

A City Where Every Corner Has a Story to Tell

But why confine art to four walls when the whole city can be a canvas? That's probably what went through the minds of the geniuses behind Ogden's vibrant street murals. Wander through the city, and you'll find splashes of color and intricate designs everywhere. Even the underpasses have gotten the artistic treatment—making your walk from Point A to Point B a journey through a visual storybook.

Speaking of stories, what about the sonic tales spun by Ogden's musicians? Whether it's the busker on the corner strumming folk tunes, or the full-throttle rock band at the weekend music festival, every note adds to Ogden's symphony of artistic brilliance.

So, let's review: we've got galleries that offer sensory feasts, streets that serve as canvases, and a musical scene that provides the soundtrack to it all. If Ogden were a painting, it would be a multi-layered, infinitely detailed masterpiece that you could stare at for hours and still find something new.

Chapter 8: "Not Just Pretty, But Smart Too!"

Brace yourselves, smarty pants and bookworms—this chapter is a shoutout to your tribe! So far, we've talked about Ogden's beauty, its gastronomy, its adventures, and its artsy vibes. But hold onto your spectacles, because Ogden is not just a looker—it's got brains to boot!

Focus on Education and Intellectual Resources

First up on our intellectual tour: Weber State University. This isn't just a place where students come to learn; it's a nexus of innovation, community outreach, and lifelong learning. With courses that range from the traditional to the cutting-edge, WSU is where Ogden's future leaders, thinkers, and doers are being molded. And let's not forget its contribution to arts and culture. With theatre productions, art exhibits, and lecture series, the campus itself becomes a microcosm of the broader Ogden community.

But what if you're past the college years? Fear not, because Ogden has a range of lifelong learning opportunities that put your typical community college to shame. We're talking cooking classes with master chefs, photography workshops in our divine outdoors, and even coding bootcamps for those looking to pivot into tech. In Ogden, the term "renaissance person" isn't an old-timey concept; it's a lifestyle!

Universities, Libraries, and Initiatives Making Ogden a Hub of Knowledge

Let's turn the page (quite literally) and head to the city's libraries. These aren't your shush-and-study zones; they're vibrant community centers.

With digital resources, interactive workshops, and storytimes that turn kids into book-lovers, Ogden's libraries are like intellectual playgrounds for all ages.

Beyond traditional institutions, the city is also home to grassroots initiatives aimed at knowledge-sharing. Ever heard of Ogden's community gardens? They're not just about growing veggies; they're educational spaces where locals learn about sustainable agriculture. There are even initiatives aimed at teaching financial literacy, environmental stewardship, and social justice. Because in Ogden, being educated means being engaged.

So there you have it. Ogden isn't just a pretty face with a rocking nightlife and a flair for the artistic. It's also a brainiac, a center of intellect, and a hub for thinkers, readers, and lifelong learners. Our next stop on this Ogden love train? We're diving into the city's festivals, celebrations, and the unbeatable sense of community that makes Ogden a city like no other.

Chapter 9: "Who Needs a Time Machine? History Alive!"

All aboard the Ogden time machine! Buckle up, because we're about to go on a historical joyride through a city that has seen it all—from the hustle of the railway era to modern-day marvels. Don't worry, no history lessons here—just juicy stories, high-stakes drama, and a few surprise cameos!

Ogden's Rich History, from the Railroad to the Present

First stop: the transcontinental railroad. Yep, Ogden was a bustling hub where East met West, and for a while, it was like the "Wild West" version of Grand Central Station. Trains chugged in from all directions, bringing in not just goods but an eclectic mix of people—magnates, laborers, and adventurers. The Union Station, now a museum, stands as a testament to those bustling times. Trust me, if those train tracks could talk, they'd be chatty as a morning radio host!

Fast forward a bit, and you'll find Ogden morphing into a military hub during World War II. A bit later? Ah, the skiing boom that turned Ogden's quiet slopes into powdery playgrounds. And let's not forget its role as a center for aerospace innovation. Seriously, from steam engines to jet engines, this city has been the backdrop to some monumental shifts.

How Ogden Played a Crucial Role in Shaping America

You might be thinking, "Okay, cool history, but so what?" Ah, but you see, Ogden's history isn't just a list of events; it's a slice of American history.

The railroads connected coasts, the wartime efforts fueled victories, and the outdoor boom redefined recreation for a whole nation.

Even today, Ogden is shaping America, albeit in subtler ways. Whether it's through sustainable initiatives that set a precedent for other cities or through a new generation of entrepreneurs and visionaries making waves, Ogden doesn't just adapt to history; it makes history.

So, the next time you stroll down Historic 25th Street, remember you're walking on the same cobblestones that saw horse-drawn carriages and Model Ts. As you sip on a local brew, realize that you're part of a continuum, a long line of Ogdenites who have always known how to make the most of their time—past, present, and future.

The past is prologue, but the story is far from over. Our final chapter will wrap up this love letter to Ogden, but don't fret; in a city like this, the adventure never truly ends.

Chapter 10: "The Ogden Spirit: Community, Festivals, & More"

Okay, peeps, we've reached the grand finale, the cherry on top, the pièce de résistance! We've seen Ogden through so many lenses: as an adventurer's paradise, a foodie's dream, a night owl's playground, a learner's haven, an artist's muse, and a historian's treasure trove. But what binds all these dazzling facets together? One word: community. Welcome to the heart and soul of Ogden!

How the Spirit of the Community Makes Ogden Special

You see, Ogden doesn't just exist; it thrives, pulsates, and flourishes, thanks to its people. It's the kind of place where neighbors know each other's names, where business owners aren't just faceless entities but friends who know your coffee order by heart. The city's community gardens? They're not just plots of land; they're where friendships bloom amid the flora. Even the dogs at the local parks seem friendlier here; it's like they've caught the Ogden spirit!

This sense of community is what makes local initiatives work, whether it's a river clean-up or a food drive. It's the invisible glue that holds together the city's mosaic of diversity, creating a culture where everyone feels like they belong.

Festivals, Parades, and Local Events That Keep the Spirit Alive

Now, how does this spirited community like to celebrate? Oh boy, hold onto your party hats! Ogden loves its festivals like a moose loves a mud puddle—in other words, a lot!

From the Ogden Music Festival that turns the town into a big dance floor, to the colorful Farmers Market, each event is a microcosm of what makes this place great. The Pioneer Days Parade? It's not just an event; it's a collective trip down memory lane, celebrating Ogden's rich past while looking forward to its shining future.

And let's not forget the special holiday festivities. The annual Christmas Village transforms downtown Ogden into a twinkling wonderland that could make even the Grinch crack a smile. Spooky haunted houses during Halloween? Oh, we got those too, and they're a scream, literally!

As we wrap up this love letter to Ogden, remember this: cities are more than just a collection of buildings, roads, and landmarks. They are living, breathing entities, powered by the people who call them home. And folks, Ogden is an absolute rockstar of a city, humming a tune of unity, innovation, and endless possibilities.

So, is Ogden the greatest place on Earth? We sure think so, but don't take our word for it. Come and experience it for yourself. After all, the true magic of Ogden isn't just in its vistas, eats, or activities. It's in the heartbeats of its people, in the laughter that fills its streets, and in the community spirit that says, "Hey, you're one of us."

Chapter 11: "Did Someone Say Affordable?"

Hey, hey, penny pinchers and budget gurus, you're going to love this! Just when you thought Ogden couldn't possibly be more fabulous, we've got one more glittering detail that will make your wallet do a happy dance. Are you ready? Drumroll, please... Ogden is AFFORDABLE! Yup, you read that right!

Cost of Living and Affordability

Let's do some real talk. Living in a beautiful, dynamic, and culturally rich place often comes with a steep price tag. But Ogden says, "Why should you have to choose between quality of life and quantity in your bank account?" And let's be honest, who doesn't love having their cake and eating it too?

Here, the housing market won't make you weep into your morning coffee. Whether you're in the market for a quaint bungalow or a spacious family home, you won't have to sell your soul to afford it. And renting? Oh, sweet summer child, the rental rates here will make you think you've time-traveled back to a more reasonable era.

What about everyday expenses like groceries, gas, or going out for a meal? Yeah, those are easier on the wallet too. Trust us, your money goes a long way in Ogden, leaving you with extra cash to enjoy all the epic experiences we've covered in previous chapters.

Why Ogden Makes Cents (and Sense!)

Still skeptical? Consider this: lower living costs mean you can actually enjoy your life rather than just get by. Take that spontaneous weekend trip to the mountains. Try out that snazzy new restaurant downtown. Sign up for that photography workshop you've been eyeing. In Ogden, you don't just survive; you thrive!

And for entrepreneurs or remote workers, the affordability factor makes Ogden a tantalizing option. Lower operational costs for businesses mean that your dreams of opening a hipster bakery or tech startup are more attainable here than in bigger cities where the rent might just break your spirit before you even get started.

So, let's break it down. We've got adventure, beauty, culture, history, community, and now affordability? Could Ogden be the real-life utopia we've all been searching for? Okay, maybe that's laying it on a bit thick, but honestly, Ogden does make a compelling case for the title of "Greatest Place on Earth."

To live in Ogden is to embrace the extraordinary without emptying your bank account. It makes cents, it makes sense, and it just might make your dreams come true.

Chapter 12: "Four Seasons, A Million Reasons"

Brrr, is that a snowflake? Or wait, is that the sound of springtime birdsong? Ah, the ever-changing tapestry of Ogden's seasons! Just like a favorite playlist that never gets old, each season in Ogden has its unique rhythm, vibe, and flavor. And trust us, there's no such thing as an off-season here!

How Every Season Brings Out a Different Charm in Ogden

Spring: A Bloom-tastic Wonderland

When the snow melts, Ogden turns into a floral dream. We're talking tulips, daffodils, and cherry blossoms that could rival a Monet painting. And the best part? Hiking trails get a makeover too, with wildflowers providing colorful accents to your outdoor escapades. Even the air smells like it's been freshly laundered!

Summer: Fun Under the Sun

Summer in Ogden is like a blockbuster movie—packed with action and a little bit of drama (hello, occasional thunderstorms!). Whether you're kayaking on the Ogden River, or enjoying an outdoor concert, the city in summer is a hive of fun-filled activity. The nights? Oh, they're as magical as a midsummer night's dream, perfect for stargazing or a moonlit hike.

Fall: A Symphony of Colors

Imagine walking through streets lined with trees dressed in their autumnal best, their leaves like confetti in shades of gold, orange, and red. Apple-picking, pumpkin patches, and harvest festivals give you that warm, fuzzy feeling only rivaled by your grandma's apple pie.

Winter: A Snowy Paradise

Do you hear that? That's the sound of skis slicing through fresh powder and the joyous laughter of snowball fights. In winter, Ogden turns into a snowy wonderland with opportunities for skiing, snowboarding, and even ice fishing. And don't even get us started on the holiday decorations; it's like the city dons its favorite sparkly outfit!

What to Expect and How to Make the Most of Each Season

If you're new to Ogden, or just passing through, it's easy to get into the swing of things. In spring, pack your allergy meds and head to the hills for some wildflower gazing. Come summer, sunscreen is your BFF. During fall, a camera is a must-have to capture the kaleidoscopic foliage. And in winter? Well, your best bet is a cozy jacket and a sense of adventure!

Every season has its own line-up of events and activities. Farmers markets, skiing competitions, flower festivals, summer camps—you name it. There's always something happening, so keep an eye on the local calendar to make sure you're not missing out on any seasonal magic.

So there you have it, folks. Four seasons and a million reasons to fall head over heels for Ogden. Each chapter of the year brings its own story, its own beauty, and its own adventures. So whatever your cup of seasonal tea may be, Ogden pours it perfectly.

Chapter 13: "Global Village: Ogden's Cultural Mosaic"

Hey there, world travelers and culture aficionados! You thought Ogden was just about mountains, scrumptious food, and vibrant festivals? Think again! Ogden is a cultural cocktail, a mosaic of traditions, beliefs, and customs. That's right—this city is as globally attuned as a well-traveled diplomat!

Cultural Diversity and Inclusivity

Ogden has layers, and we're not just talking about its geological strata. The city is home to a medley of cultures and communities that blend into a harmonious whole. Picture this: walking down the street, you could hear a fusion of languages—from Spanish to Tagalog, and from Arabic to Mandarin—all within a few blocks!

What makes this even cooler is Ogden's unflinching commitment to inclusivity. Here, diversity isn't a buzzword; it's a way of life. Community centers, schools, and public spaces are designed to be welcoming to everyone, regardless of their background. The city actively celebrates its diversity through educational programs, workshops, and, of course, fabulous cultural festivals.

A Celebration of Cultures in the World's Greatest Melting Pot

So, what does a typical year in Ogden's cultural landscape look like? Well, fasten your seat belts because it's a whirlwind world tour!

Fiesta Time!

Ever wanted to feel the pulsating energy of a Latin American carnival without the international flight? Ogden's got you covered with its lively Hispanic festivals, complete with mariachi bands, folkloric dances, and enough churros to satisfy your deepest cravings.

Lunar New Year Extravaganza

Come Lunar New Year, the city bursts into a spectacle of dragon dances, firecrackers, and mouth-watering dim sum. It's a time when red lanterns adorn the streets, and the community comes together to wish each other prosperity and happiness.

Juneteenth, Kwanzaa & Beyond

Ogden also pays homage to African and African American culture through events like Juneteenth and Kwanzaa. Imagine vibrant parades, soulful music, and stories that resonate across generations.

All the World's a Stage

And let's not forget the international film festivals, art exhibitions, and concerts that bring a slice of the global arts scene right to Ogden. From Bollywood dance-offs to European culinary weeks, there's never a dull moment in this city's cultural calendar.

So you see, Ogden isn't just a city; it's a microcosm of the world. It's a place where you can start the day with a French croissant, enjoy a Japanese sushi lunch, groove to some African drums in the afternoon, and end the night with some good ol' American jazz. All while being in the same awesome city.

If variety is the spice of life, then Ogden is the tastiest dish you've ever had. A blend of traditions, a mix of faces, and a blend of flavors—what's not to love? With open arms and open hearts, Ogden says, "Welcome to the world's greatest melting pot!"

Cultural diversity? Check. Inclusivity? Double-check. Another reason why Ogden is the greatest place on Earth? Checkmate!

Chapter 14: "Is Ogden Really the Greatest Place on Earth?"

Well, well, well, here we are, dear readers, at the grand finale of this whirlwind love letter to Ogden. A love letter that, by the way, is as diverse, intriguing, and splendid as the city itself. But let's get to the big question that's been hanging over our heads since the title of this book caught your eye: Is Ogden really the greatest place on Earth?

Weighing in All the Factors Discussed

Let's do a quick recap, shall we?

- **Natural Beauty**: Ogden offers a mountain for every mood, from the thrill-seeker to the Zen master.

- **Culinary Delights**: We've got a smorgasbord of mouth-watering options that range from food trucks to five-star dining.

- **Cool Downtown**: Hip meets history in an urban space that refuses to be dull.

- **Hidden Gems**: We've got secret spots that even Dora the Explorer would be jealous of.

- **Hollywood's Crush**: Move over, LA; Ogden's got star power too!

- **Nightlife**: Whether you want to paint the town red or enjoy a quiet evening, we've got you covered.

- **Artistic Flair**: Ogden is like a living canvas, a city bursting with artistic creativity.

- **Educational Excellence**: Brains and beauty—Ogden's got it all.

- **Rich History**: A city with a past that has shaped its vibrant present.

- **Community Spirit**: A close-knit community that knows how to celebrate life.

- **Affordability**: Living the dream without breaking the bank.

- **Four Seasons**: Like Vivaldi's classic, each season brings its own beautiful melody.

- **Cultural Mosaic**: A place where the world converges, and everyone's invited.

The Grand Reveal!

So, is Ogden the greatest place on Earth? Drumroll, please...

YES! A thousand times yes! Of course, "greatest" can be subjective, but Ogden makes such a compelling case that even the most skeptical naysayer might be tempted to pack their bags. From its stunning landscapes to its inclusive community, this city is like the Swiss Army knife of awesomeness—equipped to satisfy every need, every taste, and every adventure you might seek.

When you take a step back and look at all the facets we've covered, Ogden seems less like a city and more like an ecosystem of happiness, designed to make you wonder why you'd ever want to be anywhere else.

So, what are you waiting for? Whether you're a lifelong resident who's discovered new reasons to love your home or a curious traveler ready for your next great adventure, Ogden awaits with open arms and endless possibilities.

As the sun sets behind the mountains, casting its golden glow over the city, it's clear: Ogden isn't just a place on a map; it's a feeling, an experience, a home. It's a city that, once visited, lives on in your heart, proving that yes, it just might be the greatest place on Earth.

And that, dear readers, is the happily ever after in the fairy tale called Ogden.

Conclusion: "See You in Ogden!"

Alright, party people, adventure seekers, and future Ogdenites, we've reached the end of our exhilarating journey through the streets, hills, and hearts of Ogden. What a ride, huh? If this book were a roller coaster, we hope it would be the kind that leaves you screaming—in utter delight, of course—"Again, again!"

Final Remarks

We've laughed, we've learned, and most importantly, we've fallen in love. With a city that has it all—from majestic mountains to mouth-watering meals, from bustling festivals to quiet hidden gems. Ogden is more than just a location; it's a destination. A destination for happiness, growth, community, and maybe, just maybe, the greatest experiences of your life.

Now, let's get real for a second. A book, even one as fabulous as this, can only capture so much. The true magic of Ogden lies in living it, breathing it, experiencing it for yourself. So, whether you're a thrill-seeker, a foodie, a historian, or just someone looking for a place where life is truly lived, Ogden has a spot for you.

An Open Invitation to Experience Ogden Firsthand

So, consider this the open invitation you've been waiting for—maybe even the sign you didn't know you needed. Come to Ogden. Live it up, chow it down, hike it out, dance it off, and breathe it in. Join the ranks of those in the know, those lucky souls who get to say, "I live in Ogden, the greatest place on Earth."

Because here's the thing: This book may end, but the story of Ogden—and your story within it—has the potential for countless new chapters. And trust us, you're going to want to read—or better yet, live—every single one of them.

See you in Ogden, the city of dreams, the city of "yes," and without a doubt, the city you'll soon be calling the greatest place on Earth.

Made in the USA
Columbia, SC
06 August 2024

40057730R00024